Playing Toge

Written by Jill Atkins

Illustrated by Neil Chapman

Ama plays at the water.

Ed sees Ama at the water.

Can I play?

No.

Please?

No.

Ed sees Matt at the sand.

Can I play?

Yes, you can.

Ama sees Matt and Ed at the sand.

Can I play?

Yes, you can play.

We can all play together.